Rolf Heimann's BIZARRE BRAIN BENDERS

Hippo Books
Scholastic Children's Books
London

Scholastic Children's Books,
Scholastic Publications Ltd,
7-9 Pratt Street, London NW1 0AE, UK

Scholastic Inc.,
730 Broadway, New York, NY 10003, USA

Scholastic Canada Ltd,
123 Newkirk Road, Richmond Hill,
Ontario, Canada L4C 3G5

Ashton Scholastic Pty Ltd,
PO Box 579, Gosford, New South Wales,
Australia

Ashton Scholastic Ltd,
Private Bag 1, Penrose, Auckland,
New Zealand

First published by Periscope Press
An imprint of Roland Harvey Studios 1992
This edition published by Scholastic Publications Limited 1993

Text Copyright ©1992 by Rolf Heimann

Designed by Roland Harvey Studios

ISBN 0 590 55198 1

Printed in China

Bizarre Blurb

What is the single most important factor in making an Olympic athlete a top class competitor? Ask any of them and I'll bet they say, "Practice". They must repeat their event over and over until they do it to the best of their ability.

So, it makes sense that to keep your brain in top condition, you should give it a good workout as often as possible. That's why I have written this book, *Bizarre Brainbenders*. I hope you have fun on your way through – but try not to look at the answers! But just in case you have to look, they start on page 29. Best of luck!

Rolf Heimann

El Magnifico is about to perform his best magic trick – pulling thirteen white rabbits from his top hat. But how embarrassing! Not a single rabbit appears!

Can you find El Magnifico's rabbits?

EL MAGNIF

AND HIS
13
WHITE RABBI

② Captain Whalebone's buried treasure

This is a page from Captain Whalebone's diary:

We dropped anchor in a little bay and set out immediately to find a good hiding place for our gold. We walked through swampy ground towards a distant peak, which I called Mount Whalebone. Soon we crossed a small creek which I named Whalebone River. Not long after that we came across a smelly lake, which I called Schnock's Pond, after my first mate.

The miserable stream that flowed into it I called Schnock's Creek. Following the creek upstream we discovered a magnificent waterfall, which I named Whalebone Falls. Here is where we buried the treasure, by the light of the sinking sun, right in the shadow of a large rock above Whalebone Falls. Then we walked back to the ship in Whalebone Bay.

Looking at the old map, can you work out where the treasure is buried, and the location of Whalebone Bay?

Tile tangle

Time limit: 45 seconds

4 **F**ill in the missing letters, and find the name of two English writers. But first you must crack the code! (Clue: How well do you know your alphabet?)

7

5

Columbus capers

"Cut!" screamed film director Schomirroff. "What is the meaning of this? Where is Anne? Isn't she responsible for getting the right props for this scene? Columbus would not have worn shoes like this! This is supposed to be the year 1492, when Columbus discovered America."

The shoe is not the only thing that is wrong with the scene. There are at least twelve others that you may be able to find.

Round the twist in 60 seconds Time limit: one minute.

7 **Microchip mayhem**
Time limit: this one should take only
30 seconds!

8 Problem panels

What do these panels have in common?

9 All for one and one for all

Each of these panels could be considered the odd one out. Can you work out why?

10 Magpie mayhem

This whole town seems to be falling apart! A smug-looking magpie is stealing anything it can gets its beak around. Can you find where all the items in its nest have come from?

By the way, many of the townsfolk have dogs to scare the magpie away. How many dogs can you spot?

CLF 680

13

11 Jigsaw jumble

By transferring the jumbled lines in the left-hand grid to the correct place in the right-hand grid, you should be able to form the picture.

12 Double trouble

A two-headed snake? That is something to see! Unfortunately it has been released into the normal snakepit and is very difficult to find . . .

See the
DOUBLE-HEADED
SNAKE!

◆ 13 Round in circles

Time limit: One minute

◆ 14 Dots with a difference

Follow the alphabet – and don't be confused by the numbers!

15 **Face to face with painting**

Alberto Chiaroscuro, the famous portrait painter, went out in search of a person to paint. He much preferred painting faces to painting landscapes, but as much as he looked he could not find a person to sit for him. Luckily his imagination saw faces in everything!

How many faces would he be able to see in this landscape? Don't forget to turn the page upside-down and sideways!

◆16◆ **Circuit breaker**

Time limit: 30 seconds

17

Capital idea!

The names of 14 international capital cities are hidden in this word puzzle. See how many you can find.

L	R	P	A	R	W	A	M	C	B
I	O	O	T	T	A	W	A	A	U
M	M	N	I	L	S	C	D	N	D
A	E	P	D	F	H	W	R	B	A
P	O	L	S	O	I	K	I	E	P
B	E	R	L	I	N	C	D	R	E
L	O	P	R	A	G	U	E	R	S
G	S	N	E	H	T	A	C	A	T
L	N	A	I	R	O	B	I	P	L
W	E	L	L	I	N	G	T	O	N

18

Amazing ant-ics

There is turmoil at the ant farm! The old queen just got sick of her job, so she abdicated. The ant that first reaches the royal chamber will be crowned the new queen.

Which entrance leads to the royal chamber?

19 Zany zoo

What a shock! During the night, someone stole the zookeeper's keys and opened all the cages. He'll need some help to find all the animals: 8 monkeys, 8 snakes, 6 penguins, 5 turtles, 4 seals, 3 bears, 1 camel, 2 giraffes, 1 elephant and 1 kangaroo.

ELEPHANT KANGAROO
PENGUINS BEARS
SNAKES

ZOO

21

Left grid labels: D2, D1, B4, D4, C3, C4, E1, E3, A3, A4, C1, B2, E2, C2, C5, D5, B1, E5, B3, D3, B5, A2, E4, A5, A1

	A	B	C	D	E
1					
2					
3					
4					
5					

20 Jumbo jumble

By transferring the jumbled lines in the left-hand grid to the correct place in the right-hand grid, you should be able to form the picture.

21 Six-sided similarity

Make your way through the hexagons by stepping from the first panel to the one that shares some similarity. For example, pear to apple, apple to pumpkin . . .

22

Model city

Ella Gesson is the new fashion model for Highlife magazine. Everybody wonders where she comes from. You can find out by taking the letters from the left and putting them in a new order on the right.

 ## Bubble burster

Time limit: 30 seconds

23

24 ▷ Oddsville

"Casa Pepe – that's the oddest name for a chinese restaurant that I've ever seen!" said Mr Gibson.

"Not as odd as the food they seem to serve," remarked his wife. "In fact this must be the oddest town we've ever visited! Just look around!"

Mrs Gibson was right. The town was full of odd and crazy things – and even some things that were absolutely impossible. Can you spot them?

Today's Special:
Sauerkraut a l'Austronaut
with
Chocolate Gumbo !!!!

No Smoking
Restaurant

Dreaded diagonals

Time limit: this one is easier than it looks – no more than 45 seconds!

26

Hidden fame

The names of seventeen famous men of history are hidden in the word puzzle. See how many you know.

E	I	N	S	T	E	I	N	E	R
L	R	L	L	E	B	H	L	C	E
L	O	F	E	M	N	C	O	O	K
I	R	P	S	O	O	A	C	L	L
H	E	A	E	Z	E	B	N	U	N
C	H	S	I	A	L	P	I	M	O
R	T	T	D	R	O	F	L	B	S
U	U	E	R	T	P	A	S	U	I
H	L	U	E	W	A	T	T	S	D
C	E	R	V	A	N	T	E	S	E

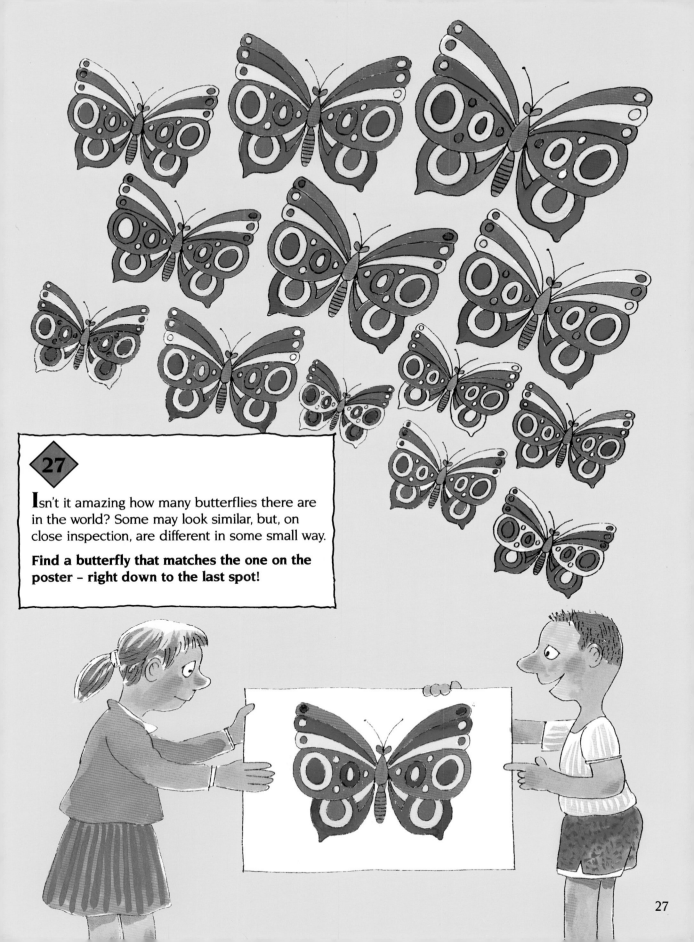

27

Isn't it amazing how many butterflies there are in the world? Some may look similar, but, on close inspection, are different in some small way.

Find a butterfly that matches the one on the poster – right down to the last spot!

28 Crazy cogs

Time limit: 45 seconds

29 **D**etective McQuick was on the track of two bank robbers. One of them had already escaped overseas and had left a note for his accomplice telling him where he had gone. The note was written in a strange code, but it took only five minutes for Detective McQuick to work out the name of the city.

How long will it take you?

The Answers

Here are the solutions to the more difficult brainbenders.
You shouldn't need solutions to the others!

1 **El Magnifico and his 13 white rabbits**

2 **Captain Whalebone's buried treasure**

3 **Tile tangle**

4 Dickens and Shakespeare

5 **Columbus capers**
When Columbus landed on American shores, there were no paddle-steamers, no lighthouses, no flag of the USA, no revolvers, no sunglasses, no cameras, no outboard engines, no wrist-watches, no baseball caps. Also, tobacco pipes were unknown to Europeans and American Indians did not have T-shirts, firearms, horses, thongs and could not yet have been converted to Christianity.

8 **Problem panels**
The number 4 is common to each panel – 4 dots, 4 masts, 4 legs...

9 **All for one and one for all**
The first panel is the only one containing red, the second panel shows the only living thing, the third panel has the only yellow background and the fourth panel shows the only object that has nothing to do with water.

Magpie mayhem

There are seven dogs.

 Jigsaw jumble

 Double trouble
The two-headed snake is the one straight down from the boy's hand at left.

 Dots with a difference

 Face to face with painting

 Capital idea!

The 14 international cities are:

Budapest	Ottawa
Madrid	Wellington
Washington	Canberra
London	Lima
Berlin	Oslo
Prague	Nairobi
Athens	Rome

Amazing ant-ics

Zany zoo

2 Giraffes

1 Elephant

8 Monkeys

8 Snakes

5 Turtles

3 Bears

1 Camel

6 Penguins

4 Seals

1 Kangaroo

 Jumbo jumble

 Six-sided similarity
The correct sequence is: pear, apple, pumpkin, skull, bones, pirate ship, steamer, whale, fountain, watering can, seedling, tree, pear.

22 **Model city**
Ella Gesson comes from Los Angeles.

24 **Oddsville**
Here is a list of things that are wrong in Oddsville:

1. The Baker's shop is called "Butcher."
2. The street numbers are out of numerical order.
3. All three clocks show different times.
4. The exit door in the toilet block leads to the river.
5. The dog has 6 legs.
6. The traffic is travelling the wrong way down a one-way street.
7. The whip and the fishing rod have swapped places.
8. The poster saying "Visit London" shows the Eiffel Tower in Paris.
9. Mohammed Ali is famous for his boxing brilliance, not his piano recitals.
10. The horse pulling the cart has a cat's tail.
11. A hose leads from the water tap to a lamp.
12. The paddle-steamer could not have fit under the bridge.
13. The paddle-steamer's smokestack is blown one way and the flag another.
14. The U.S. flag is incorrect.
15. The paddle-steamer's port light is red, and the starboard light is green (should be the other way around).
16. The chessboard should have 8 squares on each edge.
17. The man on the park bench is playing a cello that is shaped like a guitar.
18. The downpipe on the balcony of the Casa Pepe restaurant leads to a wastepaper basket.
19. The man on the balcony is holding the telephone receiver upside-down.
20. The can of yellow paint is marked "Red."
21. A man is smoking a pipe in a non-smoking restaurant.
22. Two people are playing a game that is a combination of golf and badminton.

26 **Hidden fame**

The 17 famous men are:

Einstein	Bach
Churchill	Columbus
Pasteur	Napoleon
Luther	Cook
Cervantes	Edison
Steiner	Ford
Verdi	Bell
Diesel	Watt
Mozart	

27 Here is the matching butterfly:

 Detective McQuick
If you cover the lower half of the strange letters you can read "Rio De Janeiro".

And finally, bend your brain around this one!